WHY HERE, WHY NOW?

ASSESSING RISK, WITHOUT ALL THE CLUTTER

A Field Guide

Chris Aboussafy

For Kathleen. Thank you.

Fear is the sudden realization of unpreparedness.

Chris Aboussafy

Table of Contents

INTRODUCTION

I have never been a Navy SEAL or any other super-cool badass patriot with time "down-range" in a foreign country. I have not built a Fortune 500 company, developed an app, or started a web empire out of my basement. I have never saved rhinos in Africa or dug water wells in remote villages. With great admiration, I have read about these remarkable people and their achievements.

My world of expertise is a little more unknown in its origin. This guide contains the leadership and risk assessment lessons I have learned while spending much of my career operating seamlessly in and out of plain sight with a small, little-known group of skilled professionals.

Over my 31-year career in law enforcement, I have had the privilege of serving alongside some of the bravest men and women in the nation, selflessly tackling dangerous assignments to safeguard our communities. In the final seven years of my career, I had the honor of leading an elite undercover Tactical Apprehension Team in one of the largest metropolitan cities in the U.S.

Our mission involved conducting hundreds of dynamic operations meticulously designed to last only seconds. Our objective: To swiftly create controlled chaos, allowing us to safely apprehend highly dangerous individuals. Then, immediately restore calm before blending back into the surroundings with little to no community disruption. Throughout these operations, a constant balancing act of risk assessment versus outcome-based consequences was always in motion. The success of our risk assessment principle boiled down to one thing — simplicity.

The names and events have been edited to protect identities and to not compromise tactics or operational security for the men and women who serve on these teams.

Enjoy.

PREFACE

Simplicity is the key; we all crave the straightforward version. It's not a matter of intelligence or education; it's about distilling risk assessment to its simplest form. This ensures that everyone, not just the elite, can effectively manage it. While some specific risk assessment events demand high levels of education, experience, or influence, let's be frank—those events are uncommon. Most significant events can be traced back to a seemingly small decision that was either overlooked, ignored, or made in error before snowballing into a catastrophic outcome.

Everyone must make decisions. There is risk in everything we do on a daily basis. The principle I will introduce in this book is meant to be used by everyone in all positions within an organization. What makes it unique is its simplicity. There is no title, promotion, rank, or status needed to apply the principle because it is simply – a question — **Why Here, Why Now?**

CLARITY

Across various organizations, the process of risk assessment often becomes needlessly complex. Bookshelves brim with numerous volumes advocating for elaborate frameworks, pillars, and intricate charts, all aimed at guiding professionals in their daily risk evaluations. But what if we could strip away this clutter and isolate these complexities into a pivotal question: "Why Here, Why Now?" (WHWN).

Understanding that this principle doesn't hinder innovation, profits, or operational progress is vital. Instead, "Why Here, Why Now?" (WHWN) acts as a compass, ensuring a comprehensive examination of direct and indirect risks throughout the decision-making process. Far from embracing risk aversion, this principle provides a structured approach that scrutinizes decisions without impeding the process. It grants organizations the invaluable opportunity to assess the timing of their choices, environmental factors, and potential social impact.

As the business landscape grows increasingly intricate, embracing the WHWN principle becomes imperative for enhancing risk management practices. What does WHWN entail? Let's explore the shift when my decisions went from an ego-driven, "Let's do this!" type attitude to a more critical reflection of "Why here, why now."

On an autumn morning, my team had positioned themselves discreetly outside a hotel, surveilling a shooting suspect we had tracked for the past three days. As a sergeant leading a tactical apprehension team in a busy metropolitan area, we'd conducted hundreds of missions like this over the years.

As dawn broke, our previous intelligence sources had developed the suspect's pattern of life; he'd emerge within the next two hours to take out the trash. We planned to covertly control his environment while he approached the garbage bins. Once in a predetermined area, we would initiate a tactical event that involved the use of a flashbang, environmental confinement, and speed to apprehend him. In my anticipation, I envisioned a quick resolution, eager for an early start to our weekend.

However, our plan abruptly changed in a pivotal moment, altering our strategy and reshaping our operational approach for years. It came as a phone call from our newly assigned lieutenant. While he appreciated our plan, he posed a fundamental question: Why here, why now? Initially caught off guard, having meticulously covered the logistical and threat assessment aspects, I found myself speechless as he remained silent on the line. With a moment to reconsider, I scanned the surroundings again under the new morning sun.

Across from our position was another parking lot, roughly 200 yards away, cluttered with vans stacked with baseball gear. There were no signs of activity outside the hotel, yet potentially inside were players — adults or perhaps kids — unknowns to us. What struck me was that our lieutenant, not present at the scene, wasn't aware of these vans but was prompting me to pause and reassess what I could see, but more importantly, what I could not see. My risk assessment expanded beyond the immediate threat posed by the suspect to consider the potential collateral impacts that weren't within our line of sight.

What about the shock and fear it might instill in the hotel occupants, hearing the reverberation of a flashbang and seeing a team clad in tactical gear with unmarked vehicles? What about the hotel staff, unsuspecting of the impending disruption? What is the potential fallout for the hotel's reputation and business? How might the media inquiries from the city council regarding perceived danger affect our executive staff? While our intended action aimed to ensure community safety, its broader implications were detrimental to the community fabric. So, 'Why here, why now?' transformed into a resounding 'Not here, not now.'"

For three days, we maintained surveillance on the hotel, observing the suspect pass by our parked cars, utterly unaware of our presence. Come Monday, he checked out, drove down the street, entered a convenience store, and was peacefully apprehended in the parking lot; he was armed. Opting out of our initial plan cost us the entire weekend, entailing significant overtime expenses and leading to palpable frustration within my team.

However, the expenditure proved its worth as we shifted our perspective from immediate gains to long-term returns by reframing the risk assessment. The decision to hold back took less than thirty seconds — just a moment to reassess and pause. The call to "embrace risk" echoes loudly among critics, visionaries, and innovators. It has forged remarkable achievements and even birthed nations. However, if risks are within our grasp, why not pause to assess, briefly delaying an endeavor to ensure the most suitable timing and conditions? These exacting standards extend beyond law enforcement. Consider military strategists, surgeons, pilots, and financial advisors — masters of intricate tasks, all navigating within a constant chamber of risk.

The best of these individuals instinctively applies the WHWN principle daily; their accomplishments are the foundation of their life's work. Stepping away from the realm of police tactics,

I had the fortune of encountering a diverse spectrum of individuals involved in managing businesses of various sizes. Each interaction offered a wealth of lessons.

Among these encounters was "Jerry," a seasoned entrepreneur who owned a demolition company and had initiated nine previous ventures. During one evening conversation, Jerry shared his intriguing approach to risk management in entrepreneurship, surprisingly aligning with the WHWN principle. He described a unique methodology: whenever a business opportunity arose, he'd meet the person pitching the idea over a casual coffee session. While reviewing the business model during the pitch, he paid particular attention to their level of eagerness. Intrigued, I asked why this trait held more weight than a traditional business plan presentation.

Jerry revealed greater risk in individuals displaying excessive eagerness (distinct from genuine enthusiasm), as they often fell into categories like dreamers, hustlers, or those overwhelmed by their ambitions. Contrarily, he observed less risk in individuals' content to "build it as it comes." Amidst these business conversations, Jerry discreetly assessed their justifications for applying the WHWN principle to the inception of a business.

Jerry began in farming, evolving his enterprise into a small empire with a diverse portfolio. Yet, he trusted his instincts with people more than any business pedigree. Rooted in his farming experience, Jerry understood the art of planting ideas and patiently nurturing their growth. He firmly believed that rapid growth often yielded lesser rewards in the long term; instead, he championed slow, steady progress for a higher and more sustainable yield. This philosophy extended to his approach to financial investments. Jerry continually assessed his position throughout his successful career, contemplating the right moments to venture into new endeavors. He often chose to pass on opportunities due to considerations of timing, funding, or external factors—adhering to the WHWN principles he applied to his risk assessments. He expected the same careful evaluation from those working with him.

In the realm of professions, interesting parallels often emerge. While overseeing the Tactical Apprehension Team, our annual recruitment selection process involved a rigorous three-day evaluation. During these assessments, I assigned two seasoned team members to "observe" the applicants while the rest led them through multifaceted tests. There were distinct types among the applicants — the "call of duty" enthusiasts (COD), exuding strength, speed, flashy tattoos, and better beards, contrasted sharply with the quieter, more unassuming "plow horses."

Surprisingly, the plow horse group, earnestly seeking to earn their place on the team rather than the COD crowd merely coveting the unit's insignia pin and t-shirt, captured my attention. On the surface, the dichotomy between a farming/construction empire and a tactical apprehension team seems vast. Yet, both domains applied a similar principle: WHWN? Why embark on a business venture now? Why pursue a role in a tactical unit? Investing in either type of individual had profound implications for long-term risk management. A business's success or failure could mean financial loss, while a tactical officer's error could have fatal consequences. Unbeknownst to Jerry and myself, we shared an investment mindset and utilized the same risk assessment principle in our decisions.

THE DEBT

In every risk assessment model lies a vulnerability, a potential Achilles' heel. Within the WHWN model, this vulnerability takes the form of Ego — an often underestimated yet potent force. While numerous risk management resources highlight the toxicity of ego, few genuinely delve into the self-awareness required to purge it from individual or institutional decision-making processes concerning risk. Each decision carries the shadow of a person's ego, lurking in the recesses, ready to exert its influence when the stakes are high, especially when the stakes are high. Within our team, we coined a term for events that spiraled into chaos: Ego-Driven Tactics (EDT).

When individuals or other teams fell prey to the EDT model, the WHWN framework often fell by the wayside. I don't claim a position of judgment in these instances; I, too, have been guilty of succumbing to EDT in my career. At the core of the WHWN model lies its adaptability, which is applicable at any juncture within a risk management scenario. Recognizing when the risk becomes uncontrollable and initiating the WHWN brakes often begins with an individual discarding ego from decision-making and taking hold of the brake lever.

Years ago, the department blindsided our three tactical apprehension teams with the unexpected announcement of their disbandment, abruptly reassigning us back to patrol; the team members couldn't fathom the reasoning behind this decision. Despite our unit consistently achieving high arrest numbers and riding what we perceived as a wave of success, we faced disbandment on a Friday, only to be back in uniform the following

Monday. Having joined the unit only a few months prior, I sincerely believed in our officers' mission and proficiency. Recognizing the end was near, I requested a favor with the executive command staff and secured a closed-door meeting to gain insights into the sudden turn of events.

On a Thursday afternoon, I sat with my boss's boss — well, you get the point. Armed with our team's statistics and accomplishments, meticulously compiled and presented, it might as well have been inscribed in crayon and Latin; they did not care about the statistics. Their focus wasn't on the outcomes but the methods employed to achieve those numbers. Over the years, the unit had earned a reputation for its somewhat loose tactics, and there had been some tragedy.

Now, it seemed the time had come to settle the debt. Fully aware of the incidents in question, I sat there desperately trying to think of a way to slam the brakes on this decision. In complete agreement with the assessment, I recognized that the debt was too substantial to argue. Nevertheless, I decided to go all in. I vowed the entire unit would undergo a complete transformation, not just in its tactics but, more crucially, in its culture.

My belief in the people, the mission, and its significance to the community fueled this vow. While ego had undeniably played a role in landing us in this predicament, I knew we could dig ourselves out. Despite making a plea (or maybe begging... not my proudest moment), the answer was an unequivocal... "No". Leaving that meeting, I carried the weight of letting everyone down and informed the teams that the next day would mark the end of our unit.

A few cocktails deep that same Thursday night, I received a call from one of the individuals in that closed-door meeting. The message was clear in its consequence: "If you guys don't immediately become what that team is supposed to be, then you and the other eight will not see daylight for the next five years. Tight as a drum, goodbye!" While I knew fifteen others were being reassigned, only eight were granted the chance to stay and rebuild. It was a long road for all of us to pay off the debt load.

Those eight officers resented me for the first year; I suspect three still do. However, against all odds, they accomplished the transformation by becoming the best. Eventually, our work earned another team reinstated because we stopped letting "ego" drive our decisions and tactics. In hindsight, we were fortunate that our executives prioritized quality and safety over mere numbers. Despite the unit's high arrest figures, our ego-driven tactics finally caught up with us, leading to tragic incidents and professional repercussions.

I didn't perform any magic or play any favor cards to save the unit; it was a collective effort. We re-trained, re-equipped, and reprogramed our tactical apprehension methods. What likely changed the minds of our executive staff was witnessing a newfound humility in their team. Changing the tactics was easy; the real challenge lay in transforming the culture, as it was the root of our issues at the time.

RUN IT AGAIN

Changing the culture within any team is difficult but an especially formidable challenge within a tactical team. As a team leader, I've come to recognize that altering ingrained behaviors and attitudes requires more than mere directives; it demands a profound shift in mindset and an unraveling of deeply established norms. The existing culture is often shaped by many years of shared experiences and a collective identity almost designed to resist change. Initiating transformation involves navigating a delicate balance of respecting the team's heritage while instilling a new vision.

However, there was also a tactile issue; their specialized tactics needed to be changed. It would be easy for such an elite team of officers to take offense at the department's view of their work. They had arrested murderers, cop killers, child molesters, etc., at significant risk to themselves. The team commonly boasted they went after "the worst of the worst." ... I always hated that phrase and immediately ended its use.

To me, that phrase had negatively contributed to our culture. All police officers arrest the worst of the worst, day in and day out, all over the world, whether on tactical teams, patrol squads, or detective bureaus. What makes teams elite are mindset, discipline, and decisiveness, all of which the Tactical Apprehension Team possessed, but some sharpening was needed. Before delving into how the culture changed, it's crucial to understand why individuals within this unit harbored resentment when told they needed to change. In their defense, no one had ever told them they were doing anything wrong; they were merely instructed to keep producing high arrest numbers. The unit had existed in various forms for nearly two decades, enduring multiple name changes and bounced around the department to different bureaus. As a result, the unit had collectively developed a victim-like survival mechanism. After the fourth name change and with the perennial threat of disbandment, it became increasingly challenging for team members to feel like they were part of a larger team.

They questioned whether their hard work was genuinely appreciated within the department. Despite their remarkable success over the years, a constant verbal reminder of being the "little brother" to the SWAT team (despite statistical evidence to the contrary) also contributed to the team's resistance to change. This highlights a crucial aspect of culture change—relationships. The significance of relationships in changing culture is not a departure from the WHWN principle — it is a pivotal aspect.

The initial step was bridging the gap between the Tactical Apprehension Team and the SWAT team, both now part of the same bureau. I initiated a discussion with "John," an old friend and the lead Sergeant of one of the SWAT teams. I was aiming to eliminate the big brother/little brother dynamic. Needless to say, the reception could have been warmer.

As usual, he was blunt and direct. I can remember the conversation like it was yesterday because we have laughed about it a lot since then. I sat down and said, "I need you to re-invest in my team'. He paused, started laughing, and said, "Bro, I love you, but screw that and all their bullshit. I've begged them to be better, and they want to be cowboys". He then recounted numerous prior conflicts between the two teams in the middle operations.

I reminded him that these incidents had occurred before I arrived, and our executive staff had pushed the reset button. I also reminded him he had come from the Tactical Apprehension Team before his career in SWAT, so he had helped contribute to the current culture I was trying to change … "you're such an ass." was his response.

Sometimes, a magical thing happens when two team leaders converse in a room. While one of those people points out all the wrongs one team has committed, the other team leader reaches into his pocket, pulls out a notebook book, and starts reading off the other team's forgotten missteps. Following some heated exchange, John conceded that perfection did not reside in the SWAT ranks either; it's tough when two friends know each other's jobs and faults and have kept receipts.

John finally agreed the culture had to be changed and said SWAT would help with the train-up; his teams were not happy with him, but he wasn't one to seek their affirmation on his decisions. Naturally, the notion of SWAT training the Tactical Apprehension Team went over like a flashbang thrown into a church service. Both teams harbored years of resentment towards each other for botched operations.

Though the two teams were in the same bureau, they operated differently by design. SWAT is like a giant battleship moving into position. They are designed to be overwhelming, highly structured, and methodical in their force application in a static environment. The Tactical Apprehension Team is intended to be covert, flexible, and swift in applying tactics in a fluid environment. Secretly, my intention was to give the Tactical Apprehension Team some of SWAT's greatest assets: Discipline, structure, and equipment expertise.

Conversely, I knew SWAT would take home some of the Tactical Apprehension Team's greatest assets: Increased operational flexibility, higher op-tempo, and the use of trapdoor tactics. The first couple of train-up sessions were silent and tense. However, an (un)expected transformation happened in the following weeks. Despite escalating challenges during training, the apprehension team kept pace and embraced the rigorous exercises.

Simultaneously, the Tactical Apprehension Team finally received the equipment they had sought for the past five years from their command staff: throw robots, short-barreled rifles, flashbangs, lightweight shields, 37mm impact rounds, night vision, and more. The total train-up lasted almost a year and a half before achieving full equipment readiness and being deemed 'independently operational'; this was done while still doing hundreds of apprehensions a year.

Following this, the two units now deployed together on operations; the Tactical Apprehension Team was primary on certain set factors, and SWAT on other set factors. They functioned as a cohesive entity, a remarkable sight. It was a grueling year and a half to eradicate the team's victim mentality from years of non-structured support. Now, no big/little brother dynamics existed—only brothers and sisters equally valued for their unparalleled expertise.

Initially present in both units, layers of frustration, arrogance, victimhood, and competitiveness dissipated in pursuit of a shared goal. What halted this was a shared aspiration for improvement. Even if members from both units hesitated to acknowledge it, their collaboration led to collective progress; working together brought out the best in all of them.

Once the train-up was complete, life got worse for my team, which was entirely by design. They now operated at an unprecedented level of proficiency, excelling in open-area arrests, vehicle containment techniques, and trap-door tactics; they had truly become a tier-one Tactical Apprehension Team. Instead of resting, I intensified our training regimen from bi-weekly sessions to weekly. The complaints were non-stop, but they did it; whether the temperatures were 115F or freezing, they got it done, and my words of "run it again" have been etched into their memories with life-long resentment.

Despite occasional hiccups, the team evolved continuously, setting higher operational and training standards. In addition to honing the tactics, we had to confront another challenge—ego-driven behaviors. While certainly not pervasive among all team members, it necessitated a collective accountability. Conversations with investigative sergeants underscored a recurring concern: Etiquette.

Our investigative supervisors and investigators, a pragmatic and no-nonsense group, emphasized the need for a shift in our approach. One of them, a friend, had heard of our "rebuild" and pulled me aside for a candid discussion, advising me to shut the door for some constructive feedback. Despite his comedic demeanor, his solid reputation, credibility, and ability to deliver a reality check were undeniable.

During the next thirty minutes, he meticulously listed numerous instances of "etiquette" (ego) issues with my team that irked his investigators, catching me completely off guard. He repeatedly emphasized his gratitude for the dangerous work we did for them but requested that we dial down the office theatrics around the investigators.

I interrupted him, assuring him that those days were long gone. The next morning, after personally delivering coffee and bagels to his investigative unit, it was time for a team meeting. It is essential to highlight how vital organizational relationships are when implementing the WHWN principle. As a risk assessor, you may make decisions that speed up, slow down, delay, disrupt, or even cancel operations.

When I canceled the operation at the beginning of this book (outside the hotel), an entire squad of investigators was staged at police headquarters waiting to process the suspect, car, and hotel room. Those investigators' schedules, professionally and personally, were all impacted by my decision. Tending to relationships along the entire system ensures there is buy-in when you must make a tough decision.

After meeting with my team, it was clear to everyone that we were not the most significant link in the chain; we were only one link in the very long investigative and prosecutorial chain, and the investigators were our customers. After the team meeting, "the few" were heavily checked by the majority who had not been the issue. The culture change we had been working on for the last year and a half was now a self-correcting machine. No workplace is ego-free, but when a team gets as close as possible to that goal, it becomes a thing of beauty (and not as exhausting).

ALL UNIT'S STANDBY

If the ego is the nemesis of the WHWN principle, then the cornerstone that fortifies the structure is - Patience. While the word itself might evoke images of serene, unhurried movements — often seen as slow, tedious, or preachy. Within the WHWN principle, patience becomes the most exhilarating aspect. Far from being a tool for dramatic effect or periods of contemplation, patience within this model is about creating opportunities.

In various professions, the idea of promoting patience may seem absurd. How do we exercise patience when faced with imminent danger, such as a person wielding a gun advancing toward us, a patient hemorrhaging on the operating table, or an aircraft experiencing engine failure? These examples are undoubtedly real, but they are often outcomes. While there are sudden events that demand immediate reactions, a closer examination of most situations reveals that they were avoidable, perhaps in their early stages.

This implies that little to no risk existed initially until we introduced it; did impatience play a role in creating it? In hundreds of operations involving violent individuals, our approach often involved apprehending them when they were isolated in a vehicle or a predetermined area using a multilayered action—a strategic choice always guided by our commitment to WHWN. Despite almost daily warnings from case agents that apprehending a particular suspect would likely be a critical incident, we still grounded our tactics in patience and actionable intelligence.

In all the dynamic operations over seven years, we incurred only two critical incidents and minimal force-application reports, far below national averages: a testament to the team's remarkable skillsets, but more so to the invaluable role of patience as one of our primary cornerstones.

Nevertheless, a constant struggle between ego and patience was always present. These two adversaries battled persistently within me, my team, and the Department. What became evident was that when patience won, we won. When ego won, we lost. It meant I did not do my job for my team, department, community, or profession. It happened less after WHWN came in and essentially kicked ego off the team.

Ego should be jobless today, but unfortunately, it still seems to share corner offices in all organizations. The last few years on the team taught me a great deal about patience. Admittedly, I like looking over the edge into the ego abyss, and sometimes, I tend to get a little too close. In the few years before retiring from police work, I got a new (and final) lieutenant.

"Mike" was a seasoned tactical officer and supervisor, but he also had a deep resume in investigations. When your boss has a more extensive resume than yours, it's tough to sprinkle that magical tactical dust around the office. As we worked together over the years, I admired his ability to build a team into multiple teams with multiple mission profiles. Though I was a tip-of-the-spear type of guy, he honed my ability to be patient and taught me how to create opportunities rather than hope for them. During the final years, he did more than ask, "Why here, why now?" He also reminded me (daily) how everything evolves and that sometimes evolution is uncomfortable, in all careers.

During a dinner conversation with "Jim," the Chief Financial Officer of a multinational tech corporation that had recently transitioned from privately owned to publicly traded, I dove into the recent evolution of his risk assessment strategy. As our discussion unfolded, he outlined the profound shift in his responsibilities — from being accountable solely to one owner to now navigating the complexities of satisfying the board and shareholders.

After being given a quick Economics 101 class using hand puppets, I became an "expert" in corporate governance at the table. I also gained insights into his challenges and how they mirrored my lieutenant's words on evolution. The decision-making dynamics had undergone a noticeable transformation, particularly considering the growing discord between the original entrepreneur, who had masterfully constructed the company, and the newly established Board of Directors.

The founder, once a flamboyant visionary, now grappled with restlessness and a perceived sense of irrelevance within the framework of the publicly traded structure. Despite maintaining a seat on the board, his inclination favored a leadership style akin to "let's see what happens," aka - Ego-Driven Tactics. On the other hand, the CFO, recognizing the imperative nature of addressing 'Why Here, Why Now' (WHWN) questions, sought a more strategic and risk-conscious approach. As discussions unfolded, the clash between the founder's preference for spontaneity and Jim's insistence on applying the WHWN principle became evident.

While acknowledging the allure of some ground-breaking ideas, Jim still pointed out that their risk management components needed to be aligned with the ongoing business trajectory following the recent IPO.

This misalignment led to more "not here, not now" types of discussions within the organization. However, as Jim explained, the fact that specific ideas did not immediately align with the WHWN principle did not render them unpromising in the long run; it was a matter of distinguishing between long-term vetted returns and immediate potential gains. In Jim's words, "I never dismiss them; I simply realign their implementation." Demonstrating organizational leadership, he promptly engaged the Chief Operating Officer to introduce a structured evaluation process, outlining different timelines for executing some of the original owner's ideas.

The evaluation process encompassed a range of factors, including financial implications, business valuation, personnel capacity, system readiness, societal impact, and logistical feasibility. Only after a comprehensive assessment of these projections would the organization determine the most suitable implementation timeline that aligned with the best interests of the shareholders. Jim emphasized that the company's transition to a public entity did not involve walling off the entrepreneur who had founded it. On the contrary, he was unwittingly undergoing a retraining process on the WHWN principle. The stakes were no longer exclusive to him; they now extended to the other shareholders, too. This shift reinforced the fundamental lesson: "Everyone has a boss."

INITIATE...INITIATE

A few years ago, we were looking for a suspect who had fired shots at patrol officers after fleeing an armed robbery. The suspect had also been linked to three other robberies in the last few days and was posting numerous pictures on social media posing with various firearms, some of which he had used in the robberies and the assault on the officers. Utilizing various surveillance techniques, the suspect was located at a house belonging to an associate with an extensive criminal history.

The situation seems straightforward regarding what should happen next; we assess risk and devise a tactical plan based on the WHWN principle. This was a rare time when it had to be "Right here, right now!" The suspect had vowed to shoot at the police if he saw them, and he was walking back and forth in the front yard with a rifle.

The suspect had not seen an undercover surveillance team parked in the neighborhood photographing his posturing and advising us of his actions. After a quick discussion with my Lieutenant, I decided to take him as soon as he got back into his car to leave. The house he was visiting had other known bad guys and small children living there. After three intense hours, the suspect emerged from the house, cradling the rifle under a baby blanket. As he approached his car, I gave the "all units standby" command. Anticipation hung as the suspect climbed into the car and prepared to leave. Instead of the anticipated signal, I issued a sudden "Abort...Abort! " Command.

The resulting radio silence was palpable, broken only by the eventual acknowledgment from my team, "Copy...Abort."

Something felt off; the suspect didn't start the car immediately, even though the weather was hot, and the vehicle ran. As the team held its position, my phone rang. It was a commander I had known since our days as patrol officers in the '90s. Like many others, he had been listening attentively to the unfolding situation.

Considering the heightened attention from the press, community, officers association, and the suspect's family pleading for his safety, he inquired about the plan. I told the commander I would act when the time was right. He replied, "Chris, it's your call. I'm listening." I knew what that meant. I was always referred to by my call sign at work; no one ever used my first name; it meant everyone had set up lawn chairs and had their radios tuned to the "glad-that's-not-me" channel.

The suspect sat in the car for an hour, raising the tension. Repeatedly, I kept assessing risk using the WHWN principle, knowing that ego-driven tactics could escalate the situation. Suddenly, the car moved forward and did a U-turn before stopping alongside a brick wall half a block away. Sensing the opportune moment, I issued the command, "All units standby... Initiate, Initiate." The suspect's vehicle was contained in seconds, and specialized tactics were utilized.

To everyone's relief, the suspect, taken aback and overwhelmed, complied by putting his head back and raising his hands — everyone was safe. After the operation, my lieutenant approached me, inquiring if the commander had called. I shared the details of our conversation and my response. The lieutenant chuckled, recounting that the commander had also contacted him. He replied, "Chris and I will know when it is time, and then we will do it... Thank you, sir," before promptly hanging up. The shared understanding between my lieutenant and me, built on trust in our risk assessment capabilities, allowed us to focus on the task without unnecessary interference.

Everyone has a boss, but organizational courage must start with trusting the people you place into risk-assessing positions at all organizational levels. Everyone should be asking WHWN because it protects the people, the organization, the community, and the stakeholders. To have not given the "abort" command could have led to a dire outcome or... success. In adhering to the cornerstone of the WHWN principle (patience), the secondary location became a much more predictable outcome.

It is paramount not to ignore input from people, but risk managers must have the courage to say: No; I'll call you back; I need more information; Let's do it! Trusting people to make decisions empowers them. Though there are times when the "right" person must be the one assessing the risk, those around them should be trusted to overlap when needed. Everyone has heard the statement, "I don't know what to do, let's wait until (insert name here) gets back." Many times, that may work, but did that inaction now put into motion an event that will snowball because a decision wasn't made? Whereas an empowered employee or team may make a decision that mitigates the possible rise in risk by taking action rather than inaction.

BUT... I

There is rarely a time when there is no time. The phrase, "I had no time," is often an excuse to make bad decisions, which usually comes back to being ego-driven. An old tactical mentor of mine used to say, "Time is power; keep acquiring it until you truly run out of it." In a world that has become purely outcome-based, we need to ask WHWN more than ever. Not only are there possible financial implications, but new layers of accountability have been added: Social humiliation, legal prosecution, employment sanctions, civil action, public scrutiny, riots, etc.

Some of these consequences are sometimes inevitable when making hard decisions, but most can be avoided by just taking a deep breath and asking... Why here, why now? The immense and growing industry of excuse-making has recently become a significant contributor to our Gross Domestic Product.

Excuses are usually the result of a decision that did not go as predicted. As a leader, I became angry when I was given excuses. During my evolution, I realized that my anger only compounded problems for me and the employees in the future. If you remove the anger, you soon realize excuses are often given to avoid embarrassment; the employee made a decision, but the outcome was not as planned. First, look at the outcome. The "Outcome Dial" has four spots (remember, stay simple): All Good – Bad - Really Bad - For F&*k Sakes (FFS). Let's focus on the first three. The Bad and Really Bad outcomes are not ideal but manageable.

Depending on the history of the employee, these can be learning moments. If we reach one of these two outcomes, it was because at least a decision was made, most likely not utilizing the WHWN principle, but at least a decision was made. How a leader deals with it is where the magic happens. Getting angry will result in that employee not wanting to make decisions in the future and will often lead to the "FFS" section on the outcome dial; this we want to avoid at all costs.

Within the principle, remember the importance of patience; this also applies to dealing with the outcomes. Look at the decision made and focus on how they missed applying the principle; do not focus on the outcome. It's done; it's over; clean it up, take responsibility, and move on. The magic moment is when that same employee is faced with a risk assessment decision in the future, and the outcome dial swings back to "All Good" because they followed the WHWN principle.

One of my team's responsibilities was also serving search warrants on residences. Part of the process was "scouting the location." This is when one of our team leaders goes out the day before and looks at the residence, we will be serving the warrant the following day. I had sent one of our senior team leaders to scout an apartment. They had done countless other scouts for me, and I trusted their assessments.

Early the following day, we geared up and drove to the location to serve the warrant. Except for some dim bulbs, the hallway to the apartment door was dark. We paused to ensure the team was ready, and suddenly, a voice came across my headset, "Abort... Abort... Abort;" when that command is given, there is no discussion - we abort the operation. At the command post, the heated exchange had already begun among the team while I was still walking up. I could see my team leader off to the side, staring. Once I got to the group, I learned the team leader had scouted the wrong apartment; the building numbers changed in the complex, but the apartment numbers stayed the same. We were at the correct apartment number but in the wrong building.

If the junior team member had not caught it while we were paused, the outcome would have been deep into the 'FFS' portion of the outcome-dial. After telling the rest of the team to leave, I met with my team leader. They immediately pointed out the building number issue and started inching down the 'but I...'' excuse path. My heart raced, and my blood pressure climbed...a deep breath - It was magic time.

This employee was one of the best; I needed them to keep making risk assessment decisions. We discussed how they had forgotten the "here" portion of the WHWN principle that almost led to a catastrophic event: It's done, it's over, clean it up, take responsibility, and move on.

Note: That team leader is still one of the best of the best and has never overlooked the "here" part ever again.

A couple of takeaways from that example. The junior team member realized the risk train was out of control and applied the WHWN brakes. It would have been easier to second-guess himself and acquiesce to the team leader's seniority. Still, that junior team member knew he had the power within our organization to speak up, and thank God he did. This is an extreme example of empowering employees, but as discussed in the previous chapter, there can be catastrophic outcomes for inaction. A second takeaway is I should have followed the WHWN principle myself.

Before serving all search warrants, the sergeant must also scout the location separately from the team leader, ensuring we follow the golden rule of leadership: Trust but verify. I over-trusted my team leader and did not verify the apartment's location myself. As a result, the ego-driven tactics were at full steam ahead. As stated before, when ego won, we lost. I also never broke the golden rule again.

I...

It would be easier to leave my mistakes out and raise myself as a demigod of risk assessment, but then no one would listen because everyone would know I was full of crap. Part of realizing the importance of the WHWN principle is also recognizing you have made previous decisions that have resulted in good (and bad) outcomes. During my career, I made risk assessment decisions using the WHWN principle that resulted in the loss of life, people being hurt, the destruction of property, and families being broken apart. But, as you read those examples, those results were decisions made to protect innocent people or communities; the outcomes, though severe, were needed right here, right now.

But that doesn't mean I haven't hit the FFS section on the outcome-dial myself. Many years back, our undercover surveillance team had tracked a murder suspect to his ex-girlfriend's apartment. This surveillance unit continually pulled off magic in their ability to find, follow, and set the table for our team to initiate a tactical plan... except this time. The murder suspect was staying in a lower-level apartment, which was recessed into a dark common hallway with only one other apartment. The suspect was seen wearing a baggy red hoodie and was described as 5ft 4in, weighing 350 pounds. As the sun came up, the doorway opened, and the subject came walking out to the parking lot wearing a baggy red hoodie pulled up over his head.

Both teams confirmed it was our suspect, and he was walking into our designated area of apprehension, where a tactical plan would be initiated. I had run through the WHWN principle, and everything was clear. I gave the command "Standby… Initiate, initiate". As I turned the corner of the building, the flashbang had already been perfectly placed. The suspect went to the ground and followed all commands as my team closed in. The surveillance team watched the apartment as we took the suspect into custody. Great job, best of the best…

While walking over to my team, who now had the murder suspect sitting upright, I heard a strange radio transmission from the surveillance team covering the apartment, "We have the suspect on the patio; he is complying." What…?

If they have the suspect, who is the guy on the ground? We had just gone deep into the FFS portion on the outcome dial!!! There have been a few times in my career when I felt like hyperventilating; this was one of them. I was like Harry Houdini on how quickly I got the handcuffs off… the neighbor. Yes, the neighbor, who was the same height and weight and wearing a similar baggie red hoodie. How did something like this happen? My lieutenant called me at that moment since he had heard all the radio transmissions.

I answered and said, "I need to look at this and call you back." The answer I got back is precisely what a seasoned leader should say… "Take a breath, take your time, and call me back." What had happened was a set of coincidences that had led us into the FFS zone. The doorways to both apartments were directly side by side and recessed in a dark hallway beneath some stairs. When the surveillance team saw the door open and the red hoodie exit, they called it since they were unaware of the adjacent doorway.

The person who walked out of the apartment fit the description to a tee. As the person entered the parking lot, my team identified him using all the same visual cues, except it wasn't him.

The murder suspect had heard the flashbang go off and ran onto the patio to see what was going on like a concerned citizen. At that point, he was face to face with the surveillance team who was also watching the arrest of the guy in the parking lot; they all just stood together and watched, then the "wait a minute, put your hands up!" moment occurred... I can't even make this stuff up.

Once I had all the information, I called my lieutenant back. There was a long explanation and quite a few "okays" repeated by my boss as I recounted the events. At the end of my dialogue, he asked, "First and foremost, what are you currently doing for the neighbor?" I explained that I owned our mistake and would not play the "never admit fault" game that most municipalities and businesses love to engage in (I'll return to that in a minute). I then explained that the neighbor had not been injured, just shaken up, and was very supportive of the police.

He also absolutely hated the murder-suspect neighbor and was glad he was gone. I told my boss I had given him my card, the number to our risk mitigation unit, and my cell number to call me if he needed anything. A complete report was going to be made to document the entire incident, and I also would come back to the apartment later to personally follow up with him. The phone was quiet for a long moment, and he said, "Okay, I'll call you back." I knew what that meant; this was going vertical to headquarters — time to wait. Being in the FFS zone is very uncomfortable. What I was most angry about was scaring this very nice citizen who had unknowingly walked into a situation he had nothing to do with.

Though a violent suspect was on his way to police headquarters, there was no celebration by either team. We were all embarrassed and felt horrible. The undercover sergeant (a man I greatly respect) tried to take full responsibility for the misidentification. I appreciated that, but the team applying the specialized tactics was ultimately responsible, and they also had misidentified the suspect. I sent my team away and told them we would discuss it later. They left in silence.

The phone rang, it was my lieutenant. This was the same Lieutenant who had initially asked me, "Why here, why now?" years ago. We had been through hundreds of fluid operations together since that original question. So, whatever was to come, I respected the hell out of the man who would send it my way. He started, 'Well…it went vertical. I explained everything and how it happened. They did not like it but understood it. That being said…get something into place by the end of the week so this does not happen again".

In the following four days, we tested and ordered new infrared optics for the teams. We also established that an identification could not be made unless the face was uncovered entirely and visible; if that meant more surveillance for hours or even days, then so be it. I said I would get to the "never admit fault" that most municipalities and companies' pound into their employees. As I sit and preach the WHWN principle, we cannot forget how to own an outcome. The City's risk mitigation officer immediately ensured we looked after the citizen and did not shy away from owning our FFS moment. The Department acknowledged the entire event and documented everything to a tee, not once inching anywhere towards 'never admit fault.' That accountability went a long way with that citizen and their family.

It would have been easy to say that I was not part of the identification and trusted the multiple officers giving the positive ID; start bubble-wrapping my career as soon as I knew we had flash-banged ourselves deep into the FFS zone. Even when originally recounting the events to my boss, he had asked who had given the wrong identifications and thrown the flashbang. I told him it was me that did everything. He knew what I was doing and left it at that; it didn't matter who did what at that time; what mattered was we were looking after the citizen and owning our mistakes, and he completely understood that.

Two other tactical supervisors and I had lunch with my Lieutenant a few days after that incident, and we went over it in fine detail. I also heard our executive command's wording as they were briefed on the incident. While eating, he also explained that he told them something else. I sat there while he chewed, and then he finally spoke, "I want you all to know while Chris was briefing me, he never used the word (they), only the word (I)." He wanted me to know that the explanation resonated with our chain of command and mitigated their response.

He added that if he had initially heard me use the words, "but, they…" he would have immediately kicked me off the team; he wouldn't be able to trust my risk assessments anymore because he knew they would always be based upon the best outcome for me, not the organization or community. The WHWN principle is not about the risk assessor. It is about the bigger picture, even the portions that cannot be seen. If we make decisions based on what is best for us, then we are not assessing risk; we are assessing our self-preservation.

Imagine if your heart surgeon utilized self-preservation risk assessment; nobody would be in the operating room; your pilot would never leave the ground; your groceries would never arrive at the store; nobody would do anything because there is risk in everything. This is one of the cruxes of the WHWN principle; it focuses on others. Within organizations, there are times when admitting fault would cause far more devasting financial outcomes or brand damage. Yet, there has been a growing trend in the "own it, and move on" method of outcome-based responses: When there is nothing to uncover or crusade against… it becomes boring, and people move on.

HOW MUCH LONGER

The outcomes don't need to be severe or grandiose to apply the WHWN principle. Every situation is different, and the speed at which they come at you is different. The foundation of the principle is its simplicity. "Do I grab a chocolate donut before I go into a board meeting while wearing my new white dress shirt?" ...pause, assess... WHWN... not here, not now. Another? Okay. "Do I have a couple more beers before I talk to my boss at the Christmas party?" ... WHWN... pause, assess... not here, not now. Easy.

The point of these scenarios is to bring things back to earth; neither risk assessment in those two incidents required us to review a matrix, tenants, silos, or pillars; four simple words resulted in the right action and decisions that potentially saved professional embarrassment.

So, as you prepare to throw this field manual into the top drawer of your home office or turn the audiobook off, what do I want you to take away from the WHWN principle? That risk is not something to fear or even shy away from. Bring it on!! Risk assessment and decision-making are fun and empowering. We have all survived a decision and asked ourselves, "How the hell did I live through that?" The old saying, "Bad decisions make great stories," is entirely accurate. At the cocktail parties or fire pits, most people are not trying to entertain with stories of self-serving grand accomplishments; the best stories usually start with, "So, there I was …". Bad decisions can be entertaining once they are put into perspective.

Except, there are those other ones, the…FFS. Countless employees have made decisions that have hit the first three stages of the outcome-dial and have become high performers. Even those who have overachieved and hit the FFS portion of the outcome-dial can still be saved and turned into high performers with a couple of exceptions: Is there a pattern? Is the damage too significant? What message am I sending to my other employees?

Almost the last example… I promise. We were training on the range one day and utilizing flashbangs within the scenario. After the training, I saw my team leader slam his truck door and walk away from the group. I told everyone, except my team leader, to gear down and hit the street. After everyone had left, he explained that someone on our team had been trying to place the pin back into a flashbang he had not thrown. A flashbang (aka NFDD) is a small handheld explosive that is thrown into an area/room to temporarily overwhelm a suspect's senses for apprehension or area denial. Once the pin is pulled, it is not something to play around with, or you will blow your hands off.

When a flashbang's pin has been removed and is not used, it is to be thrown into a safe area, and a "bang-out" warning is yelled. Here is a little background on this team member with the flashbang. He is a friend, and I have known him since we were baby officers on patrol in the 90's. He had come to the team, and everyone knew we were friends and had a lot of history together. He is a great police officer and a great family man. I told my team leader I would deal with the issue, and he flatly responded, "Okay, boss." I knew my team leader felt an exception would be given due to my relationship with the teammate. I called my boss and ran the facts by him.

He, too, was friends with this team member since the '90s and said, "Well, this is going to be your call on which way this goes, rehab or removal. I will support your call." I went home that night, and I did not sleep. I knew I could rehab him, and he would be successful. That was the plan.

The next day, we met out on the street. I rolled down my window (took a deep breath) and said, "Effective immediately, you are non-operational. Effective Friday, you will be removed from the team and assigned to patrol." When I told him that, he could not see that my hands were shaking below the windowsill of the SUV. There was some silence, and he responded, "There was no other option, boss; you have to kick me off.

I respect you for that and knew you would make the right decision." Wow…to this day, that hurts to write, but that was an impressive display of accountability from him. That moment sucked! The night before, I had come up with every excuse not to remove him, but none of the outcomes followed the WHWN principle. The mistake was too grave, and to retain him would've meant I was lowering our standards and could cost me my credibility as a leader with my team.

The decision was clear once all the clutter was removed: Not here, not now…you're gone. The point of this example is that though I preach the magic teaching moments for leaders and supervisors, there are times when the eject button must be pushed. The organization, the employees, the shareholders, the community, and your teammates expect organizational courage. I have watched, too many times, how supervisors have retained employees out of friendship, guilt, or because they lacked the fortitude to kick employees off teams. Whatever the reason (usually weakness), it rarely has an excellent long-term outcome.

Now, before anyone starts reciting some story of a "unicorn employee" who was given a second chance and is now the CEO, please take a deep breath. As you recall, I pointed out specific considerations when it comes to a wrong decision made by an employee: Is there a pattern? Is the damage too significant? What message am I sending to my other employees? When a supervisor is sitting alone and trying to decide the fate of an employee, they are assessing risk utilizing the WHWN principle.

The short-term relief of letting someone know they still have a job may feel good at the moment, but as that employee walks out the door, the supervisor has now placed a big red stamp of approval on them; any future outcome caused directly or indirectly by that employee will have the supervisors' stamp all over it. So, does this mean it is safer to be soulless and risk-assess human beings as we would a robotic floor sweeper? Yes.

It is safer. Yet, it is not possible. Emotions always take a seat in decision-making, especially when deciding someone's livelihood. I used a simple rule to help me make those hard decisions. Over 27 years in my department, I had five supervisors who embodied what it meant to be a great leader and a great manager (it's very rare to be both).

I would envision myself making the same wrong decision the employee in front of me made. I then would ask myself, "Would those five people remove or rehab me?" As a side note, two of those people have kicked me out of past positions. When I conducted this reverse-role analysis, I could still hear one tapping her pen on the desk, another breathing heavy sighs, and another repeatedly asking me, "Seriously, Chris, seriously?". It is just an analysis that has worked for me and seems to have a high success rate. The number can vary - mine happens to be five.

You get paid to risk-assess situations, people, places, and tasks… so do your job. Sometimes, managing human beings sucks because most of them are great people. That does not mean they belong in their jobs. Police departments are famous for randomly putting people into jobs where they do not belong, and it usually means disaster unless truckloads of bubble wrap are dropped off daily. Hell, I didn't belong in a few jobs I had over the years.

Early in my supervisor career, as a new Field Training Officer (FTO) Sergeant, my Commander quietly walked into my office before he headed home one day and said, "Chris, you are a horrible FTO Sergeant. You start plain clothes neighborhood crimes, Monday." That was it; nothing else was said. He just walked out the door, and I was transferred on Monday. Thank God for all those new patrol officers and their senior trainers because I was horrible at that job, and he knew it... so he dealt with it swiftly and with sterility; I always respected him for that.

"Do your job! … they don't need another friend; they have friends." This was something one of those five great leaders said to me repeatedly. I agree with it for the most part. I was never known for my hugs, candies left on people's desks, or sticky notes with words of encouragement. Everyone who has worked for me is completely laughing at the thought of me doing any of that. That said, you can "Do your job" as a leader while recognizing that actual human beings work for you.

Nothing reminded me more of that daily than the thirty seconds of radio silence after the "Initiate, Initiate" command was given on tactical apprehensions. All those seconds add up and take a massive toll. It also reminded me of my deep connection with those men and women on my team. I always tried to flex their time off so people could be at kids' soccer games, help sick spouses and pets, take mental health days, etc. Conversely, they also understood my decisions were always made in the best interests of the community, the department, the profession, and them. Finding that balance is the secret in any organization; when it's personal, it's not business. When it's business, it's not personal.

That final sentence is overused, but I've found it to be true. When I had to remove people, they knew it wasn't personal (even if they didn't like it), but they knew it was a sterile decision. Years ago, I ran into someone who had previously worked for me on a high-performance team; they had since been promoted and were doing a great job as a supervisor. While waiting for a meeting, he turned to me and said, "I never liked you very much, but I would have followed into anything because I respected you. But I didn't like you."

I told him that was one of the highest compliments a leader can receive… and that I never really liked him either. It reinforced that being respected as a leader or a decision-maker had a much more profound impact on people than being liked. If that same employee had liked me but not respected me, they would not have followed me out of the precinct parking lot. As a risk assessor, strive to be respected and liked, but if you must choose one, be respected. I never did ask him why he didn't like me.

This leadership model goes against what is being taught in today's leadership classes. I understand the needle has moved towards the "servant-leader" and the gentle workplace. I wish police departments would adopt some of those principles; I know their employees would benefit. With that in mind, pause the new leadership styles being taught and consider how both styles transpose. As I mentioned before, I tried to be very flexible regarding personal requests from my employees so long as it did not impact our operations. I did not do it to be liked or for servitude credits. I did it because it fell into the same WHWN principle as everything else, and it made the environment – consistent.

The week I retired, I was talking to a member of my team who had been with me since the first day I started. I joked about how lucky they were to finally get rid of me after all these years. We laughed, but the officer said the team would miss my "predictability." As we chase the newest way to be a leader, we always seem to be coming back to the same time-tested techniques: Be fair, be honest, be competent, be consistent and be predictable. Since adopting the WHWN principle, my predictability became rock solid. Since I was no longer using my ego to make decisions, most decisions I made were completely predictable, making the team's work environment better.

FINALLY

So, there are no more examples, just the handing over of the magical risk assessment tool because everyone likes closure. This won't take long because the past sections have already given you the foundation. Some may think, "Okay, but where is the actual answer?" to WHWN. The answer is the one that comes to you after you take that single breath and exhale all the ego, nuances, emotion, exhilaration, and repercussions; it is - That - Answer.

This is where other authors unintentionally insert clutter, adding to the confusion. The human brain is a fantastic computer because it simultaneously processes various information sources such as social optics, operational fatigue, managerial support, emotional responses, and other subtle details within your organization. The answer to Why Here, Why Now? is already waiting to be verbalized when the decision is made.

We tend to fail when we lack the courage to make the decisions already on our tongue that our brain has already vetted. I am a proponent of repetition training, so I will leave you with some homework. While walking around the office, store, house, or street, make mundane decisions through the same question: WHWN? Soon, you will begin to answer the questions quicker in your head without the ego-driven answers creeping in. I try to do it when considering another late-night Amazon purchase or "upgrading for a dollar more." As we previously discussed, these are minor risk assessment scenarios, but they are practice for when the big situation comes.

There is a reason my team ran through the same training scenarios hundreds of times over the years: when it counted, they were the best risk assessors I knew. I realize people want simple formulas for decision-making; nowadays, they ask their phones or AI for life direction. If organizations try to fire up the fifty-slide PowerPoint or throw the 400-page book on the desk, employees will not watch or read it. Boring! We all despise charts, matrixes, silos, lanes, platforms, formulas, blah, blah, blah.

The last thing anyone wants to hear is, "Turn to page 203 and follow chart 2.2 to assess this risk and make a decision." Give people the most straightforward tools to deal with problems, simple or complex. As you prepare to head out into the fast-paced world of risk assessment, remember not to be distracted by all the bright lights and shiny objects. Remember, the obvious answer is found by asking the most straightforward question: Why Here, Why Now?

It seems too simplistic, right?... It works. Or... cuddle up in a warm blanket and grab that 400-page risk assessment book (20 of those pages being referenced material along with 30 quotes from dead military leaders and Roman emperors) and spend the next 20 hours memorizing (or never finishing) ... Boring!!

Well, I guess that's it. I will hold myself to the WHWN principle and end this field guide, "Right Here, Right Now," to avoid losing your attention.

Run it again...

ACKNOWLEDGMENTS

I want to thank all the people listed in this book. Even though their names were changed, they know who they are. Specifically, I want to thank the amazing men and women who worked for me, with me, and in support of all of us. It was a team environment where, at times, we fought like brothers and sisters on the front lawn but were unbreakable when it mattered. I want to thank the command staff who did not accept mediocrity and pressed the reset button. Specifically, the last Lieutenant I had who asked the one question that set in motion an evolution in the way decisions were made, making us all better... Thank you, sir.

I also want to thank Paula, Noah, Josh, Harry, John, Tammy and Brad for your friendship and contributions to getting this done. To my wife Kathleen, who is always there and never gives up on me, I love you.

To the Teams... Thank you for trusting me.

ABOUT THE AUTHOR

Chris Aboussafy's law enforcement career spans over 31 years in Canada and the United States. In 1995, he was hired by a department in one of the largest metropolitan areas in the United States, where he worked for 27 years.

During that time, he worked various assignments, including patrol, plain clothes neighborhood enforcement, and the investigations bureau. After promoting, Chris oversaw two federal undercover task forces targeting Mexican cartel gun buyers and drug interdictions. He later supervised a deep-cover unit focusing on prison and motorcycle gangs as well as white supremacist organizations trafficking weapons and stolen property.

Chris transferred to the Tactical Bureau to supervise the Department's elite undercover Tactical Apprehension Team for the last seven years of his career, conducting hundreds of dynamic operations in fluid environments. After retiring, he founded Bishop One LLC, focusing on field-tested and statistically backed pre-emptive tactical training specializing in Trapdoor Tactics™, Vehicle Containment Techniques, and Open-Area arrests.

These courses are designed to reduce force application responses with limited community disruption, increase community trust, reduce civil liability, and curtail unnecessary SWAT deployments. Chris has also lectured on "Intel-Driven Tactics "at a large university and is planning presentations on risk assessment, decision-making, leadership, and team-building principles to various organizations.

To contact Chris Aboussafy:

chrisaboussafy@bishoponetraining.com

www.bishoponetraining.com

Instagram.com/bishoponetraining